STARSIDE ELEMENTARY

GALAXY OF SUPERSTARS

Ben Affleck
Backstreet Boys
Brandy
Garth Brooks
Mariah Carey
Matt Damon
Cameron Diaz
Leonardo DiCaprio
Céline Dion
Tom Hanks
Hanson
Jennifer Love Hewitt
Lauryn Hill
Jennifer Lopez
Ricky Martin
Ewan McGregor
Mike Myers
'N Sync
LeAnn Rimes
Adam Sandler
Britney Spears
Spice Girls
Jonathan Taylor Thomas
Venus Williams

CHELSEA HOUSE PUBLISHERS

GALAXY OF SUPERSTARS

Matt Damon

Meg Greene

CHELSEA HOUSE PUBLISHERS
Philadelphia

Frontis: *No matter what talented screenwriter and actor Matt Damon accomplishes, he has promised himself to never forget who he is or where his roots are.*

Produced by
21st Century Publishing and Communications, Inc.
New York, New York
http://www.21cpc.com

CHELSEA HOUSE PUBLISHERS

Editor in Chief: Stephen Reginald
Managing Editor: James D. Gallagher
Production Manager: Pamela Loos
Art Director: Sara Davis
Director of Photography: Judy L. Hasday
Senior Production Editor: J. Christopher Higgins
Publishing Coordinator/Project Editor: James McAvoy

The Chelsea House World Wide Web address is
http://www.chelseahouse.com

First Printing

1 3 5 7 9 8 6 4 2

Library of Congress Cataloging-in-Publication Data

Greene, Meg.
   Matt Damon / by Meg Greene.
      p. cm. — (Galaxy of superstars)
   Includes bibliographical references and index.
   Summary: A biography which describes the unusual childhood and early interest in acting of Matt Damon, the popular young actor who wrote and starred in "Good Will Hunting."
   ISBN 0-7910-5779-8 (hc) — ISBN 0-7910-5780-1 (pb)
   1. Damon, Matt—Juvenile literature. 2. Motion picture actors and actresses—United States—Biography—Juvenile literature. [1. Damon, Matt. 2. Actors and actresses.] I. Title. II. Series.

PN2287.D255 G74 2000
791.43'028'092—dc21
[B]   99-086662
                                                                        CIP
                                                                        AC

CONTENTS

1

"TRY TO ENJOY THE MOMENT"

In early February it is still dark in Los Angeles at 5:30 A.M. Having to accommodate the early morning talk shows on the East Coast, however, members of the local media, grumbling about the hour, scurried to find seats inside the auditorium of the Academy of Motion Picture Arts and Sciences in Beverly Hills. As the journalists and commentators took their places, studio publicists gathered to start the press conference. This affair wasn't just any Hollywood extravaganza. February 8, 1998, was an important day in the motion picture capital. It was the day that nominations for the 70th annual Academy Awards, the film industry's highest honor, were to be announced. That year, actress and Oscar-winner Geena Davis and the president of the academy, Robert Rehme, made the announcements.

For Matt Damon, a young Harvard-educated actor, the results were nothing short of astonishing. Along with his childhood friend and fellow actor and writer Ben Affleck, Matt had not more than a week before walked off with a Golden Globe Award for Best Original Screenplay for the

---

With their Oscars in hand, Matt and his best friend, Ben Affleck (left), clown around while posing for photographers. The young duo astonished the film world by winning the Best Original Screenplay award for Good Will Hunting.

Nominated for an Oscar for Best Actor for his role in Good Will Hunting, *young and relatively unknown Matt faced stiff competition from four veteran actors: Robert Duvall (back, left), Peter Fonda (back, right), Jack Nicholson (front, left), and Dustin Hoffman (front, right).*

film *Good Will Hunting*, the story of a young math prodigy caught between two worlds. (The Golden Globes are annual awards given by the Hollywood Foreign Press Association to honor achievements in both film and television.) At the Oscar ceremony, it was as if the Golden Globes were repeating themselves. Matt was nominated for the same two awards: Best Actor and Best Original Screenplay with Ben Affleck. In the Best Actor category he was competing against veterans Jack Nicholson, Robert Duvall, Dustin Hoffman, and Peter Fonda. To complete this unbelievable story, *Good Will Hunting* was nominated for seven more awards, including Best Supporting Actor for Robin Williams, Best Director for Gus Van

Sant, Best Supporting Actress for Matt's former girlfriend Minnie Driver, and the sweetest, and most unexpected, plum of all: Best Picture. No one, not even the executives at Miramax, the film company that took a gamble on the two young writers and actors, could have dreamed that the project would enjoy such tremendous success.

For the 27-year-old Matt, the experience was overwhelming. Prior to the nomination announcements he jokingly quipped, "I don't care if we're nominated for best morons, because I'd think, well, I got nominated with Ben, and that's pretty cool." When the ringing of the telephone awakened him, and he first heard the news of his nomination, Matt was almost at a loss for words. "Oh, boy. No, man, it's too much. Definitely too much. I can't even comprehend this," he told one reporter. To another he said, "I am staggered just to have two nominations, one with my best friend and another in the company I am in. . . . I can't even comprehend this. I already win, just being nominated."

The Oscar nominations were only one of many exciting developments in Matt's career. In the brief span of six months, Matt, a native of Massachusetts, had emerged from the pack of struggling young actors to become one of the hottest A-list stars. It hadn't been an easy road, however. At one point, Matt was ready to call it quits with acting altogether. What was happening to him at this point in time went far beyond his wildest dreams.

"I'm so happy for the movie—nine nominations!" an excited Matt later said. "I was really happy for Gus, and Robin, too." When asked if he and Ben had thought at all about being nominated for the Oscars, Matt admitted, "We thought a little about it, but we stayed really busy, which was good. We never really talked about it." Right after the nominations were announced, though, Matt agreed that both he and Ben were "shell-shocked. I called him and he just said, 'Wow. We're nominated as screen-writer.' It wasn't like we were screaming on the phone. It's like someone gives you an honor, and you're like, 'God, I really hope I can live up to this.'"

At the same time, Matt also gained a sense of perspective about his accomplishments. When he called his family with the news, his mother, Nancy Carlsson-Paige, asked if another film, *The Boxer,* had been recognized. Matt said that the film was not nominated, and his mother asked, "How can one movie get nine nomina-tions, and a totally profound movie like that get none?" He laughingly recalled what happened next. "And I said, 'But Ma, it was my movie!' and she said, 'I know sweetie, but it just makes me really mad.'"

Matt's elation over the nominations was soon eclipsed. By early March, with the awards ceremony just three weeks away, a series of rumors began to circulate throughout Holly-wood. One rumor suggested that Matt and Ben had not really written *Good Will Hunting,* and the script was the work of another writer from whom they had bought the story; another rumor declared that the two had turned to vet-eran screenwriter William Goldman to write the script. Amid all the controversy arose the most potentially damaging charge of all—*Good Will Hunting* had originally been staged as a one-act play. If this were true, then the nomi-nation for best original screenplay would have to be declared ineligible.

Matt sought to set the record straight. As far as the gossip about buying the story was concerned, Matt admitted that he had bought the title of *Good Will Hunting* from a friend in Boston who had written an unpublished novel of the same name. He also confessed that William Goldman had offered advice when the script was in its early stages but explained that Goldman's contributions were minimal: Goldman had spent one day with Matt and Ben, making suggestions on how to revise and improve the script. Matt categorically denied that the film had originally been staged as a one-act play. The closest *Good Will Hunting* had ever come to being produced was when Matt and his classmates acted a few scenes in a theater workshop at Harvard. Until it had been bought as a screenplay, it had never been ready to be published, much less performed.

Such explanations notwithstanding, it was still worrisome to Matt and Ben that the rumors persisted. After winning the Golden Globe for their screenplay, they ended up losing out on two other awards—the Writers' Guild Award and the Screen Actors' Guild Award. Despite his claims that winning didn't matter, Matt wanted a fair chance at the Oscars.

No one really knew how damaging the rumors were. Informed speculation from veteran observers of the film industry had the screenplay for *Good Will Hunting* as a two to one favorite over the other nominees. Still, no one could be sure of the outcome, and the rumors certainly didn't help. The Oscars always have a way of being unpredictable.

Monday, March 23, found Matt and Ben dressed in their evening best and escorting the

Matt and Ben arrive with their mothers at the 70th Annual Academy Awards. Matt's mom, Nancy Carlsson-Paige (right), distrusts the film industry but is proud of her son's accomplishments, advising him to "try to enjoy the moment."

women closest to them—their mothers—to the awards ceremony at the Shrine Auditorium in Los Angeles. Matt's mother attended with mixed emotions. She had always distrusted the film industry, believing that people lost track of their values and placed too much emphasis on celebrity, fame, and wealth. Nevertheless, despite her negative beliefs about Hollywood, she was pleased to witness her son's success.

Also in the audience and cheering for Matt and Ben was Matt's brother Kyle, his wife, Lori, and Matt's father, Kent. Scattered throughout various living rooms in Los Angeles were groups of relatives and friends who had flown in to be a part of the festivities. Both Ben and Matt, though nervous, were thrilled to attend as nominees and presenters in such glittering company. (They would present the award for

Best Animated Short Film and Best Live Action Short Film.) When reporters asked him once more about his chances, Matt calmly answered "I already won. People say that all the time, but watch me not win, the smile will not leave my face, I promise you. This is the most unbelievable feeling—I'm going to the Academy Awards."

True to form, the 70th Academy Awards ceremony had its share of surprises. With the blockbuster film *Titanic* predicted to win in almost every category for which it had received a nomination, the audience was stunned when the Best Supporting Actor Oscar went to Matt's costar Robin Williams. At the L Street Tavern in Boston, which was featured prominently in the film, the bar crowd, dressed in formal attire, cheered and shouted at the announcement. Any recognition of *Good Will Hunting*, many felt, was also a triumph for them. Momentarily speechless after winning the award, Williams thanked his young costars, quipping, "I still want to see some ID." Backstage, Williams, in a more serious moment, told reporters that of his four Oscar-nominated performances, the one he gave in *Good Will Hunting* ought to have won.

Matt's youth also provided a source of humor to the host of the Oscar ceremonies, Billy Crystal. Before announcing the winner of the Best Actor Oscar, Crystal joked that Matt "must feel like he's playing on the seniors' tour" (a prestigious golf tour for older professional golfers). As the audience waited with mounting anticipation, the winner was finally announced: Jack Nicholson for *As Good As It Gets*.

As disappointed as Matt undoubtedly was not to have won the Best Actor Award, he consoled himself with the knowledge that the award for Best Original Screenplay was still to come. Despite general agreement that Matt and Ben had a good chance, the competition was daunting. *Good Will Hunting* was going up against *Boogie Nights, Deconstructing Harry, As Good As It Gets*, and *The Full Monty*. The tension grew as the presenters read down the list of nominees, and clips from the films were shown. When Jack Lemmon opened the envelope and revealed the winner, the audience roared.

Matt and Ben hugged each other and their mothers. Then they hugged the set and crew members seated around them and rushed to the stage to claim their prize. Rules limited winners to making only 30-second acceptance speeches, but in their excitement, the two childhood friends did not want to forget anyone who had made their achievement possible. They thanked everyone from their families and friends to cast and crew, Miramax executives, and the people of Boston. They concluded by saying that "Whoever we forgot, we love you and thank you very much." Patrons at the L Street Bar, including the mayor of Boston, thundered their approval. Even the audience at the Shrine Auditorium was caught up in the enthusiasm of the moment.

After the ceremony, in the backstage crush of reporters, photographers, and well-wishers, Matt and Ben tried to answer questions. "I said to Matt [that] losing would suck and winning would be really scary," Ben explained. "And it's really, really scary." Ben went on to remind those gathered that "Matt and I thought we could raise a little money and make the movie. . . . we never thought it could go through the regular Hollywood channels."

For his part, Matt just looked stunned.

When asked if he would rather have won Best Actor or Best Original Screenplay, he simply replied, "Are you kidding me? I've never been here before. I didn't care."

"He just wanted a job, sir," joked Ben.

Matt, however, did remember his mother's advice—to "try to enjoy the moment."

As overjoyed as Matt was at that moment, he wanted more than just an instant of fame and glory. In his mind he had only begun to make his mark on the film industry, to taste the fruit of his labors. The morning after he won his Oscar, Matt woke up as one of Hollywood's "Golden Boys." The question was: could he sustain the incredible momentum?

Matt was overjoyed when veteran actor and star Robin Williams (shown here with Matt in a scene from Good Will Hunting*) joined the cast. Williams had nothing but praise for the script and commended the young writers when he told them "you guys really did it."*

STARSIDE ELEMENTARY

2

"THAT'S THE WAY IT'S ALWAYS BEEN"

With a population of just over 100,000, Cambridge, Massachusetts, is a medium-sized city with a small-town feel. Settled in the 1630s, Cambridge is known around the world as the home of Harvard University and the Massachusetts Institute of Technology (MIT). Almost every neighborhood has a bookstore, a bar, or a café where students, professors, workers, and professionals mingle. Cambridge is also famous for its freewheeling atmosphere in contrast to its commonly-perceived-as-stuffy neighbor Boston. For a youngster like Matt, Cambridge provided an intellectual and creative environment; it was the perfect place to grow up.

However, the Cambridge influence would come later. Matthew Paige Damon was born in Boston on October 8, 1970, the second son of Kent Damon and Nancy Carlsson-Paige. Matt's father worked at a number of different occupations, including income tax consultant, realtor, and stockbroker. According to Matt, his father's main business was real estate. Kent Damon specialized in raising corporate funds to finance the construction of low-income housing projects. After retirement, Kent

---

Boston, one of the oldest cities in the country, is Matt's beloved hometown. It was also the setting for Good Will Hunting.

Damon took on the role of baseball coach for a high school team in a neighboring town. Nancy Carlsson-Paige, a professor of early childhood development, taught at Lesley College, a small teachers' college located in Cambridge. She has never been shy about expressing her extremely liberal views on everything from childcare to politics to Hollywood. Her opinions have helped to make Matt more aware of a variety of social problems. Matt has described his mother as "a very radical lady."

For the first few years of Matt's life, home was on Bennington Street in the small town of Newton Corner, not far from Cambridge. Unfortunately, irreconcilable differences about how the Damon household ought to operate led to the divorce of Matt's parents in 1972, when he was two years old. Looking back on that time, Matt has explained that "my dad had this *Leave It to Beaver* [a popular television program of the 1950s] idea of how life should be" in which the father went to work and the mother stayed at home, cleaning the house, doing the laundry, preparing the meals, and raising the children.

Matt's mother found such a life unpleasant and extremely stifling. The eventual result, as Matt said, was that the marriage "didn't work out." The divorce, however, was friendly, and Matt's parents remain on good terms with one another to this day.

It was Nancy who had the most definite ideas about how Matt and his older brother, Kyle, were to be raised. She forbade them from playing with toy guns and other toys simulating weapons. She limited their exposure to television, especially to violent cartoons. "My mother had written some books on war play and those cartoons that are like commercials for action figures," Matt explained to an interviewer. "What worried my mother about these shows was not only that they encouraged violent play but that they also hampered creativity."

Instead, Matt's mother insisted that her sons learn to amuse themselves by using their imaginations. As a result, Matt got an early start at being creative. Sometimes, though, Matt didn't like the options available to him. He admitted to another interviewer that "growing up for me was like you'd get some blocks and then you'd have to make up a game. In our house, we only had blocks to play with. My brother and I hated those blocks." But big brother Kyle always came through. "Kyle would make these really amazing costumes which I'd wear and we'd act out these stories. . . . [T]hat was really cool. I used to think I was a super-hero." Matt's mother has vivid memories of these games as well. "He wore a superhero towel around his neck day in and day out for a couple of years," she recalled.

Matt's passion for acting the part of a super-hero sometimes got him into serious trouble. Once, convinced he could fly, Matt climbed to the top of a jungle gym in a local park and, yelling "Shazam!," jumped off. The four-year-old landed awkwardly on his ankle and broke it. Yet, if any good came out of this incident, it was, as Matt put it, that "my desire to become an actor may have started there."

Perhaps that dream actually started in the summer of 1977 when the popular film *Star Wars* was released. Matt and Kyle saw the movie 25 times. "We went nuts . . . couldn't get enough of it," Matt admitted. "It was this world of total imagination that was suddenly right

Matt tips a ball during an All-Star Celebrity Hitting Challenge at Boston's Fenway Park in 1999. As a boy, Matt loved to play baseball, claiming he was the best pitcher on his Little League team.

there in front of us. I was always acting out these parts."

For the time being, however, young Matt was not thinking about an acting career. Rather, he wanted to be a professional athlete. He became involved in sports at an early age, playing Little League baseball and practicing his basketball moves for several hours every day. By the time he was 12, Matt decided he wanted to play in the National Basketball Association (NBA) like his idol, Nate "Tiny" Archibald, who played for the Boston Celtics, his favorite team. Matt continued to practice almost obsessively, hoping to achieve his goal, until the day his dad sat him down for a talk.

Kent pointed out to Matt that his "favorite basketball player, Tiny Archibald, is called 'Tiny' because he's 6' 1", and I'm the tallest Damon to ever evolve and I'm 5' 11", but I'm never going to play in the NBA." Matt saw what was coming. "He made it clear basketball wasn't going to pan out for me too well," Matt recalled. "So at twelve, I hung it up. I gave up basketball and at that moment went into acting, instead. With the same kind of passion. I decided, I'll be an actor."

Before Matt's heart-to-heart talk with his dad, though, two events occurred that had an important impact on his life. In 1980, when Matt was 10 years old, Nancy decided to move her family from Newton Corner to Cambridge. Along with five other families, she bought a rundown old house located on Auburn Street, near the Central Square of Cambridge and situated approximately halfway between Harvard and MIT. The house was to serve as an experiment in communal, or shared, living. Decisions in the house were made by committee, and household tasks were everyone's responsibility. Each family had its own apartment and shared a common living room. Everyone in the house participated in holidays and celebrations.

Matt described his unusual living arrangement to an interviewer this way: "Everyone had their own apartment, but the kids felt free to wander." He added, "Everyone had their space and as a kid it was heaven. If your mom was out or not in the mood for you, there was always another mother who was." Some people questioned whether such arrangements were suitable to raising children. However, Matt believed, "This was a much more practical arrangement."

Although the house itself was in very poor condition when the families moved in, Nancy remained optimistic. She thought that everybody could work together to do the repairs necessary to make the house habitable. Matt and Kyle were no exceptions, and they also had to work. "My mom put little masks on me and my brother, gave us goggles and crowbars, and we [demolished] the walls." Matt recalls the experiment working pretty well. "It was governed by a shared philosophy. . . . Every week there was a three hour community meeting, and Sundays were workdays."

Nancy had other reasons for wanting to move the family to Cambridge. Instead of attending the local public school in Newton Corner, Matt and Kyle could enroll in the Cambridge Alternative School (now known as Graham and Parks), which was more progressive in its curriculum.

Nancy also wanted her sons to meet many different kinds of people. Although Cambridge had a relatively small population, an extremely diverse group of people lived there; it was home to men and women from more than 82 countries. In addition, the house on Auburn Street was situated near a halfway house, and the street itself was frequented by many homeless people. Nancy was determined that Matt and Kyle were not only going to be exposed to people from different cultures, but to men and women of different social and economic backgrounds as well.

"It was a great way to be raised, especially for an actor," Matt expressed later. "Lots of different perspectives, just surrounded by lots of positive human beings." The constant interaction between the persons of different ages and social classes and the exposure to a wide range of cultures was not wasted on Matt. As he grew older, he often drew ideas and inspiration from his unusual upbringing to shape his writing and acting.

The second major event in Matt's life was a lot more exciting. Not long after moving into the new neighborhood, Nancy Carlsson-Paige became friends with Chris Affleck, a sixth-grade teacher at nearby Tobin Public School. Chris and her husband also had two sons, Ben and Casey. The Afflecks lived in a house just two blocks from Auburn Street. The two women's friendship eventually led to the meeting of 10-year-old Matt and eight-year-old Ben.

Based on their first few meetings, no one would have guessed that the two would eventually become life-long friends. Matt remembers that he was "being pretty much forced into hanging out with Ben." However, the boys soon found that they shared two common interests and passions: Little League baseball and acting. In a short time, they became inseparable. In an interview Matt explained the basis of their friendship: "We grew up in the same neighborhood, playing the same games and experiencing the same things. If one of us had enough money for a candy bar, then the candy bar was bought and split in half. That's just the way it's always been."

By the tender age of eight, Ben was already a neighborhood celebrity for having appeared in the PBS television production of *The Voyage of the Mimi*, the story of a young boy who traveled on scientific expeditions with his grandfather.

Matt, also seriously bitten by the acting bug, continued with his classes at Weelock Family Theater in acting and pantomime (acting without words), which he had been attending for two years. Both of Matt's parents strongly encouraged him, believing that acting was a wonderful outlet for his creativity. "My mom and dad thought being in theater workshops with other little kids was a healthy thing. . . . They kept encouraging me to do it, really do whatever I wanted. That was their theory: Just be happy."

In the meantime, the two friends continued to play baseball. Matt claims that he got one up on Ben by becoming the "best pitcher in the league." Although smaller and younger than Matt, Ben was regarded as the more outgoing of the two. Not that Matt was shy—it was common to find him at crowded Harvard Square on weekends, break dancing for change tossed by amused passersby.

By the time Matt was 14, he and Kyle were attending the Cambridge Rindge and Latin School, where he earned a reputation as a diligent, hardworking, and gifted student with a desire to succeed at everything he did. As Ben said, "Matt was an ambitious student in a mediocre program." He jokingly continued, "Matt was the kind of guy who brought in a lot of apples for his teachers, if you see what I am getting at."

Handsome Matt, who was usually busy with his studies and school athletics, did not go unnoticed by the girls. With his blond hair, blue eyes, and good looks, Matt had few problems finding dates. Casey Affleck, Ben's brother, remembered that Matt "was the guy who always sat in the back of the bus making

out with his girlfriends."

But it was Ben with whom Matt often chose to spend his time. They spent nights at each other's houses, hung out at the local video arcade, or went to the movies. "I think we just look at the world in the same way," Matt once commented. "We did everything together, from Little League to chasing girls but from a very early age, what we focused on most was acting."

Two years later, in 1986, Ben also entered

The deep friendship between Matt and Ben began when they were just little boys. They bonded through their enthusiasm for acting but never imagined how far their passion would take them.

the Rindge and Latin School, and the two friends both attended the theater classes taught by Gerry Speca. Under Mr. Speca's direction, both boys received invaluable training for their professional careers—careers that they were coming more and more to think they were destined for. "Ben and I owe everything to him," Matt has said of Speca on more than one occasion. Ben agrees, saying Mr. Speca "taught kids self-discipline—how to take responsibility for themselves."

Gerry Speca remembers Matt well. Recalling Matt's first stage appearance as a samurai (a Japanese warrior) in a Kabuki (a type of Japanese theater) play, Speca described him as "this little dervish, running around, rehearsing his part, all his moves, making sure everything was just right."

Though two years older than his best friend, Matt already found himself laboring in Ben's shadow. Ben's experience as an actor often won him the bigger roles in school productions. In 1984, even before he arrived at the Rindge and Latin School, Ben had gotten another television role in an ABC afterschool special, *Wanted: The Perfect Guy*. Although Matt was pleased at his friend's success, he was becoming increasingly frustrated at his own lack of progress and bad luck. At 16, he was still performing in children's theater and attending open auditions, but nothing was happening. He could not have guessed that his luck was about to change.

Matt's first real break came later in 1986 when he and Ben went to an open audition for a television commercial for TJ Maxx. The casting director selected both boys to appear in the spot. Ben saw the job as just another paycheck. For Matt, however, it represented something far more important. It was the first time that he had been paid for doing what he loved the most—acting. He received $200 for appearing in the commercial, and because of the paycheck, Matt really began to think of himself as a professional actor. All he had to do was convince his parents to allow him to pursue his dream.

3

"THEY NEVER TOLD ME
I COULDN'T ACT"

"I announced to my mom and my dad that I was ready to go pro, as if I were a baseball player. They were just baffled," recounted Matt about the day he proclaimed his desire to pursue an acting career. Nancy Carlsson-Paige couldn't believe what she was hearing. "Did I raise you?" she asked. "That's just an egomaniacal pipe dream. How does [acting] help other people?" Ben Affleck tried to step in and come to the aid of his best friend. "I remember . . . trying to convince Matt's mom that not everybody in Hollywood was a total liar or scum. . . . I now realize it was a complete lie."

Although not at all pleased with his chosen career path, Matt's parents at last relented. They gave him their permission to go to New York to meet Ben's agent but insisted that he pay his own way. Two hundred dollars richer after having finished the commercial shoot, Matt readily agreed to their terms.

The next few weeks found Matt and Ben carefully planning their journey. "This trip was a big deal," Matt

---

Matt and his mother, Nancy Carlsson-Paige, celebrate his Best Original Screenplay Oscar for Good Will Hunting. *Although concerned about the business practices of the film industry and the prospect of an acting career, Matt's parents never questioned his talent and drive.*

remembered. "So Ben and I took the train to New York and he introduced me to his agent." Unfortunately for Matt, any dreams he may have entertained about having an influential agent represent him soon evaporated.

"I walked into the office with all this confidence, and here we were the two chumpiest kids in the world. It was like this Mom and Pop agency and they didn't even know who Ben was." Despite these initial missteps, the agency eventually agreed to represent Matt, but that was where it ended. Matt returned to Cambridge thinking he had representation and that his career was about to take off. The agency, however, never called Matt for one single acting job of any sort.

Matt continued with his studies and his acting in school productions. He and Ben got together nearly every day for what they called "business lunches." As Matt explained it, "We would take our cheeseburgers and sit down at a table . . . and we would talk business. Even though there was nothing to talk about!" Greatly amused, Ben agreed, laughingly adding, "We were really nerdy."

Matt's parents worried a great deal about his career decision. At one point in time they did try to talk to him about the many difficulties he would most likely encounter if he continued to pursue acting. "They advised me that acting was a brutal profession," Matt later recalled. "They told me, 'People are going to lie to you, take advantage of you and there aren't going to be any jobs for you.' But they never told me I couldn't act."

Despite his parents' serious apprehensions, Matt eagerly continued to participate in various school productions and made the rounds of countless auditions. Finally he got a lucky break. Matt beat out Ben for a small part in the 1988 film *Mystic Pizza*, which featured a then relative newcomer to the movies, Julia Roberts. Matt's part was very small, delivering only one single line: "Mom, do you want my green stuff?" But for Matt, it was a very real beginning. In his mind he had finally broken through. Even his skeptical mother, who attended the filming session, was beaming with pride as she watched her son perform before the cameras. Not long afterward Matt landed another small role as an extra in the film *The Good Mother*, which was also released in 1988.

Meanwhile, there was still schoolwork to do and, with graduation not far away, college to think about. Matt's first choice of colleges was Columbia University in New York City, which was followed by 10 other major schools. He was ready to leave home and be on his own for the first time. Just to comfort his mother, he agreed to apply to the local university down the street—Harvard—while making it very clear that it was definitely not his first choice. Anyhow, in Cambridge everyone knew that Harvard rarely took "locals."

When the totally unexpected letter arrived informing Matt that he had been accepted to Harvard, he suddenly forgot all about the other college applications. Harvard was just too prestigious to pass up, even though it meant that he would still have to call the Auburn Street house "home." Matt later admitted that, actually, a part of him "was afraid to leave home."

Matt entered Harvard in the fall of 1988, declaring English as his major. His mother and he agreed that he could live in a dorm on campus. Matt quickly immersed himself in his class work and also continued to pursue his acting. He hadn't forgotten about Ben, either. The two stayed in close contact by phone and in person. The new college student passed on to his younger friend many of the things he was learning in his college theater classes. Sometimes, Ben would come to campus and sit in on Matt's classes so he could hear firsthand what was going on.

Matt auditioned tirelessly for any acting jobs he could find. By this time, he had signed on with another talent agency, and as a result, he was finding more work. Success had its disadvantages though, for the more time he spent rehearsing and acting, the less time he had to devote to his studies. His demanding schedule required balancing school and acting jobs, which soon proved to be exhausting.

Life as such was filled with its share of disappointments and humiliations. Once Matt attended a meeting with a man whom he believed was the head of a major motion picture studio. "I told everyone I was going to meet the president of Walt Disney," Matt recollected. "So I go to New York but it turns out I'm not meeting the president—it's just an audition for the *Mickey Mouse Club*, complete with ears. Then I had to go back to school and everyone was asking how the audition went. . . . Ben and I still talk about that. And I didn't even get the job either."

The situation changed dramatically in the fall of 1989—the beginning of Matt's sophomore year at Harvard. Matt learned he had won a role in a film titled *Rising Son* to be produced by Turner Network Television. In the

movie he was to play the part of the son of the main character, who was played by veteran actor Brian Dennehy. For Matt, it meant being absent from Harvard for an entire semester. He would have to work extremely hard to make up for the classes he would miss if he hoped to maintain his perfect 4.0 average. Deciding whether to stay in school or accept the long-awaited offer of a movie role proved much more difficult than Matt expected. In the end, he followed his heart, accepted the role, and

Balancing acting opportunities with classes at Harvard was a huge challenge for Matt. However, he loved life on campus and described his years at Harvard as "amazing."

temporarily left school to begin filming.

The set of *Rising Son* turned out to be another kind of classroom for Matt. Working alongside veteran actors Piper Laurie and Brian Dennehy, the young aspiring actor listened carefully and watched intently. This was his biggest role to date, and he was determined to make the most of his opportunity.

When filming ended, Matt returned to classes at Harvard and anxiously awaited the premiere of *Rising Son*, scheduled to air in July 1990. He wondered whether the film and his part would be well received. He needn't have worried. *Rising Son* won critical acclaim, and critics singled out Matt for special praise. They characterized his performance as "affecting." Even more gratifying was the assessment of his talent by costar Dennehy. "He's a bright, smart, sensitive kid," Dennehy commented. "And he's hardworking. But he's got one thing that's rare and important—he's disciplined. . . . His self-control makes him different in a town that sometimes rewards you for bad behavior."

Matt couldn't have been more pleased. However, he had missed being a student more than he thought he would and was glad to return to classes. He continued to sign up for acting courses and work on university theater productions, but the experience of working on *Rising Son* made Matt realize that he really wanted to work in film. He liked stage work but recognized that it was in the movies where he felt most comfortable and could, therefore, do his best work.

The young hopeful didn't have to wait long before landing his next role. Along with Ben, Matt was cast in the 1992 film *School Ties*,

the story of a Jewish boy named David Greene, played by Brendan Fraser, who attends a snobbish prep school. Once there, David decides to keep his background a secret after discovering the anti-Semitism prevalent among his classmates. *School Ties* served to showcase the talents of a number of up-and-coming young actors, including Fraser and Chris O'Donnell. Matt played one of the antagonists of Fraser's character. When the film was released it earned good reviews but was only a modest success

Matt and Brian Dennehy (right) played son and father in Rising Son. *Even though Matt's performance received special praise from critics, his career did not take off as he expected.*

In the 1992 film School Ties, *Matt (front center) worked with young actors such as Brendan Fraser (front left), Chris O'Donnell (back right, standing), and child-hood friend Ben Affleck (back right, sitting). He was extremely disappointed when the role did not lead to more job offers.*

at the box office. Still, Matt had thought that *School Ties* would help to advance his acting career.

Things did not develop as he had hoped. After *School Ties*, Matt lost out on two other major roles to his costars from that film. Chris O'Donnell was cast in *Scent of a Woman*, and the role in *With Honors* went to Matt's friend Brendan Fraser.

Matt became extremely discouraged about his prospects. He remembered his parents' warnings about the brutality of the acting profession. It didn't help his mood when one morning Matt awoke to learn that the crew was filming a scene from *With Honors* outside his dormitory at Harvard! As Matt described it, the situation quickly went from bad to worse. "I walk out to go to my class, I'm late, and somebody says to me, 'Excuse me, don't walk through here. . . . We're filming a big movie here. . . . That you're not in.' I was just like going, *'Nooooo!'* inside. It was awful."

By the fall of 1992, Matt was in his final year of college. He continued to work hard at his studies and enrolled in a play-writing class. Matt had never fancied himself a playwright but thought the writing exercises would be good for him. One of the class assignments was to write a one-act play. Taking to heart the advice to "write what you know," Matt went to work on a story about students and "townies," as the local residents in Cambridge are called, and how their lives are often unintentionally intertwined.

The story didn't really go anywhere, but Matt still received strong words of praise and encouragement from his professor, who advised Matt to rewrite it as a full-length play. Matt gave serious thought to the suggestion. When Ben, who had moved to Los Angeles, returned to Cambridge for Christmas, Matt showed the work-in-progress to him. Together they acted out a scene from the play for one of Matt's acting workshops.

Before Matt had a chance to really revise the play, however, he received news that auditions were being held for a new movie called *Geronimo: An American Legend.* When he heard the details of the film and the possible part he could get, he knew he had to try his hardest and do his best to win the role. Two of his idols, actors Robert Duvall and Gene Hackman, had already signed on.

Matt went to New York and read for the part. One of the greatest Christmas presents he ever received was the news that he had won the role and would be spending his spring semester filming in Moab, Utah. Matt was sure that this would be it—his break-out role.

Matt threw himself into the part of Second Lieutenant Britton Davis, even learning how to ride a horse, something that most kids growing up in Cambridge, Massachusetts, don't do. After the completion of the location filming in Utah, Matt went to Los Angeles to shoot some interior scenes. While there, he visited Ben. It was like old times as the two friends talked and strategized about their careers.

Advance word was that *Geronimo* would be a box-office smash. With the promise of a block-buster hit, Matt decided it was time to take a serious gamble on his career. Although he had only two semesters left at Harvard to receive his degree, Matt asked for and received an extended leave of absence. He reasoned that if the film did as well as everyone was predicting, he would be

In Geronimo: An American Legend, *Matt got to work with two of his idols, actors Robert Duvall and Gene Hackman. Feeling certain of success, he quit Harvard and moved to Los Angeles.*

spending his time pouring over scripts rather than textbooks. He had enjoyed his years at Harvard and had learned a great deal. "Let me tell you I loved Harvard," he later said. "It was like a huge, huge part of my life. My time at Harvard was amazing." However, it seemed that the time was right to make a change. Matt took what he thought to be the next logical step. He moved to Los Angeles and took up residence with Ben in his tiny apartment. He knew it would be like old times—only better.

4

GOOD WILL HUNTING

Once again, things didn't turn out as well as Matt expected. The critics were absolutely brutal. *Geronimo: An American Legend* not only bombed at the box office, but the reviews barely mentioned Matt's performance in the film. It was all too depressing to think about. Matt refused even to consider returning to Cambridge, however. Instead, he camped out at Ben's apartment where, as Ben's brother Casey recalled, he "sat around, ate Cheerios, and played video games." Despite the setback, Matt continued to attend auditions and track down leads for possible movie roles. With the exception of a role in the Tuner Network Television production of *The Good Old Boys* in 1995, however, the next two years proved to be lean ones for Matt.

In between going to auditions and playing video games, Matt occupied himself by scribbling in a notebook. Feeling like he and Ben "couldn't get arrested" because no one appeared to be interested in them, Matt was determined

---

When working on The Good Old Boys, *Matt Damon (second from left) enjoyed working with established stars such as Tommy Lee Jones (second from right) and Sam Shepard (far right). But after this movie was produced, Matt found himself out of work. In desperation, he and Ben Affleck spent months revising the script for* Good Will Hunting, *hoping to make a film of their own.*

to do something to bring about a change of fortune. "All we got to look at were the scripts that everyone on the short list passes on," Matt said in an interview. "Then it's you and everyone else brawling for these meager table scraps."

By 1994, Matt and Ben had had enough. "We finally said, Why not just make our own movie? We'll raise the money on our own, and it doesn't matter if no one sees it, 'cause when we're feeling bad, we can put this videocassette in and say, 'That's a contribution that we made for this field that we love.'"

At this time in his life, Matt was battling personal demons as well, wondering if he'd made the right choice about the direction he had taken—specifically, he wondered whether he'd done the right thing in leaving Harvard before earning his degree. "I felt like I had given up college and all these great experiences," he admitted. "All my friends had graduated. I had missed out on a lot and here I was back at square one living in L.A. It was really a horrible feeling." The main question Matt asked himself was what he could do to improve his outlook and his circumstances.

Since arriving in Los Angeles, Matt had, on and off, continued working on the play he had written while at Harvard. A year later, without other prospects at hand, he and Ben turned to it in earnest. They decided to work together to convert the play into a script for a film. "Cowriting was the only option," Matt concluded, "because I didn't have the discipline to sit in front of the computer and wait for something to happen. . . . I definitely wrote out of frustration and desperation—Ben and I wanted to create work for ourselves because we couldn't get hired as actors."

Surviving on Spam, Cheerios, and Ramen Noodles, Matt and Ben worked on the script through the spring and summer of 1994. By the time they had finished it, the script was more than 1,000 pages. They didn't know any film writers from whom to seek advice about what to do next. Although they believed in their story, they wondered what they ought to do with the finished draft.

At last they agreed to take the script to Matt's agent. "He read it out of a feeling of total obligation—and probably dread," Matt attested. "But he really liked it." In fact, Matt's agent liked the script so much that he took it to another agent, Patrick Whitesell, who was equally impressed. Whitesell met with Matt and Ben and suggested something that they couldn't believe. Why not try to sell the story to a studio, Whitesell said, instead of struggling to make the film themselves?

Matt and Ben had never, in their wildest dreams, imagined that a major production studio would consider their screenplay. But on Sunday, November 13, 1994, to their total surprise and delight, the script of *Good Will Hunting*, as the story was now being called, went on the auction block. There was one condition they had: whichever studio bought the screenplay would have to agree to cast both Matt and Ben in starring roles.

"When the phone started ringing, we were ready to take the first [offer], which was $15,000," said Ben. Matt recalled that "after each call, we were yelling at our agent, Patrick Whitesell, '*Take it. Just take the offer!*'" Some studios were interested in the script but not in casting Matt or Ben. At this point, they were so excited that anyone wanted their script, they didn't care. If no one agreed to their terms, they could fall back on their original plan of financing and making the film on their own. They were, for the time being, simply overwhelmed by all the attention the script was generating among film industry executives.

For four days, the studios negotiated the purchase of *Good Will Hunting*. Matt and Ben spent their time either waiting by the phone or meeting with interested studio personnel. Matt understood that "people certainly weren't like, 'Let's get these two knuckleheads to headline our movie.' And they certainly weren't going to pay a lot of money for it and then give away the best two parts to us." Ben added, "The really sort of outrageous thing was that nobody knew who we were. They said, 'This is great; we think we could get some really good actors for this.' And we're going, 'No, no, no—we're the actors.' And they were like, 'Oh, you're the actors? That's sweet. That's cute.'"

One studio offered one million dollars if Matt and Ben would step away from the script and sell the story outright. Their response was immediate and final: No! "We never once thought about taking the money and running," Matt affirmed. He did admit, though, that "we were afraid . . . it was going to fall apart."

Then, just as suddenly as the bidding war had begun, it was over. By Friday, Matt and Ben had agreed to make a deal with Castle Rock Entertainment. Castle Rock paid the two writers $600,000 for the rights to the script of *Good Will Hunting* and agreed to give them the two starring roles with certain conditions. "They [gave] us so much . . . money, we didn't even know what to do." Matt and Ben celebrated with their friends in a low-key style over cans

of warm Pabst Blue Ribbon beer and a $6.99 all-you-can-eat shrimp dinner at a Sizzler Steakhouse. For the first time, Matt felt he had some control over his career, or as he put it, "like I finally won a round."

Shortly before they offered the script for *Good Will Hunting* to the studios, Matt learned that he had won a role in the 1996 film *Courage Under Fire*, the first major production about the Gulf War, starring Denzel Washington and Meg Ryan. In the film, Matt portrayed a young soldier who becomes addicted to heroin. Still flushed with the success of selling the script of *Good Will Hunting*, Matt turned his full attention to his newest role.

To make his character more believable, Matt decided to lose weight in order to portray the physical effects of drug addiction. Instead of

Matt with Meg Ryan in a scene from the 1996 film Courage Under Fire. *To prepare for his role as a heroin-addicted soldier, Matt lost nearly 40 pounds.*

going to a doctor to monitor the process, Matt chose to lose the weight on his own. His efforts were frighteningly successful. He lost almost 40 pounds and, although he made it through the filming, he became terribly ill.

The determined young actor thought the sacrifice would be well worth it, whatever the consequences to his health, if film critics and studio moguls took favorable notice of his performance. Again, he was very disappointed. Although *Courage Under Fire* got good reviews and Matt himself received some complementary notices in addition to praise from Denzel Washington, the recognition he craved still eluded him. Matt became so discouraged after the release of *Courage Under Fire* that he was ready to give up acting altogether.

Meanwhile, to make matters even worse, the prospect of actually making *Good Will Hunting* was growing more remote. There was a problem about the location of the film. Castle Rock wanted to film in Canada to reduce its expenses. But Matt and Ben insisted that the film had to be shot in their hometown, Boston. Between rewriting the script and negotiating with the studio, Matt and Ben were not having an easy time getting their story ready for the screen.

By 1996, the script was in "turnaround," which meant that Matt and Ben had 30 days to sell their script to another studio and repay Castle Rock's development costs or the studio would assume full ownership of the rights. Matt and Ben were horrified at the prospect. If they could not find another studio interested in buying the script and willing to pay them enough to refund the expenses Castle Rock had incurred, then Castle Rock would gain the exclusive right to do whatever it wanted with

Good Will Hunting, including making the movie without Matt and Ben or not making it at all.

Matt and Ben knew they needed help and needed it fast. Three days before the deadline Ben contacted a director named Kevin Smith with whom he had recently worked. Ben persuaded Smith to read the script. The next day Smith contacted Ben and gave *Good Will Hunting* a favorable review. Smith then called Harvey Weinstein, the co-chairman of Miramax Pictures, suggesting that Weinstein purchase the story from Castle Rock. Once Weinstein looked over the script, he quickly agreed. He offered Castle Rock just under one million dollars for the rights to *Good Will Hunting*—the largest amount Miramax had ever paid for an original screenplay.

Once Miramax acquired *Good Will Hunting*, the first decision that needed to be made was who would direct the picture. Much to Matt and Ben's astonishment, actor/director Mel Gibson expressed strong interest. However, due to prior commitments, Gibson could not begin work on the project for almost a year. The studio then selected Gus Van Sant, who was available immediately, to direct the film. Matt and Ben couldn't have been more pleased. Both were big fans of Van Sant's work and felt assured that he would do justice to their story. Van Sant was equally complimentary, calling the script "probably the best-written screenplay I had ever read."

Even though Matt was busy revising the screenplay for *Good Will Hunting* with Ben, he still found enough time to read for the part of the young idealistic lawyer, Rudy Baylor, in Francis Ford Coppola's upcoming project *The Rainmaker*. By the summer of 1996, he was on

Matt Damon and costar Minnie Driver enjoy a romantic moment in Good Will Hunting, *in which Minnie plays Matt's love interest. The couple had begun dating seriously even before Minnie signed on for her role.*

his way to Memphis, Tennessee, to begin filming. This could be another big break, Matt thought. If he did well in this role, it could not only open other doors but might also help to promote *Good Will Hunting*. Matt was right. His being cast in Coppola's film provided the final push to get *Good Will Hunting* into production.

In their few spare moments, Matt and Ben labored to put the finishing touches on the script. By early 1997, after going through two studios, 10 rewrites, and countless sleepless nights, everything was finally ready to proceed. Only one major question remained: who would play the important role of the psychiatrist?

This matter was settled one day when Van Sant casually mentioned that he had cast Robin Williams as the psychiatrist who helps

Matt's character, Will Hunting, cope with his problems and his genius. Matt nearly fell out of his chair at the news. "I couldn't believe what I was hearing. I didn't think things could get much better." With Robin Williams in place and actress Minnie Driver, Matt's then real-life girlfriend, signed to play Matt's love interest in the film, the cast and crew were ready to get underway.

As Williams had only five weeks before his next film project began, his scenes were shot first. The entire cast and crew moved to Boston, where the film takes place. Matt would never forget the first day on the set. "By the time they said 'action,' tears were running down my face. I looked over at Ben, and he was the same way. Then right after the scene, Robin came over and put his hands on our heads and said, 'It's not a fluke; you guys really did it.'"

5

"ACTING ... THAT'S WHAT I DO"

As quickly as it had begun, the shooting of *Good Will Hunting* came to an end. When the filming was finished, Matt found himself with mixed feelings. "I realize I'm not going to get up and go to work. . . . There's a little sadness there. But at the same time, it feels good to have [*Good Will Hunting*] done."

Not being one to rest on his laurels, Matt was already eager to begin his next film project, *Saving Private Ryan,* starring Tom Hanks and directed by Steven Spielberg. Matt's role in this drama about D-Day (the day the Allied forces first landed in France during the Second World War) came about by accident. Robin Williams had invited his good friend Spielberg to watch a day of filming for *Good Will Hunting.* Spielberg, who was in Boston making *Amistad,* was so taken with Matt that he decided on the spot to cast him as the title character.

Matt concedes that Williams "dragged me along" to meet Spielberg. "I met Steven, who had seen me in *Courage Under Fire* but didn't realize I had lost 40 pounds for that job and didn't always look like a skeletal junkie. A week

From left, Tom Hanks as Captain Miller, Matt Damon as Private Ryan, and Edward Burns as Private Reiben are poised for action in this scene from Saving Private Ryan.

later I got the Private Ryan part."

The new role was another dream come true for Matt. *Good Will Hunting* was turning Matt's life into a whirlwind of activity. From the time he began filming, Matt embarked on one of the busiest schedules in Hollywood. After a brief vacation, Matt flew to England in the summer of 1997 to begin filming *Saving Private Ryan.*

By the fall of 1997, when Matt returned to Los Angeles, Hollywood was abuzz. Matt's performance in *The Rainmaker* was getting solid reviews; *Good Will Hunting* was in theaters and playing to appreciative audiences and critical acclaim. People in the film industry were beginning to take notice of the young actor.

At the same time, Miramax began touting *Good Will Hunting* for possible Oscar nominations. Every movie critic and journalist, it seemed, was calling to set up an interview with Matt, whose face appeared on the cover of two popular magazines, *Interview* (with Ben) and *Vanity Fair.* Matt enjoyed the attention he received, but he was a little unsettled by it as well. "It's like I'm living someone else's life. . . . if people are expecting this much, will they be mad if I let them down? I don't want to be a flash in the pan. I don't want to lose it all."

Someone else also worried about Matt. His mother was not at all happy with the amount of media exposure he was getting. She feared that Matt was being exploited or manipulated by the press. She was particularly disapproving of his appearance in *Vanity Fair*, for she regarded the magazine as trivial and characterized it as nothing more than "two hundred pages of ads for things that people don't need." "I'm not happy about it," she complained. "My beautiful boy is on the cover. . . . He's not a

human being anymore. He's become a product that people can pick up and judge. . . . I worry about that—how it will affect him."

To his credit, Matt was also concerned about the sudden exposure and notoriety. One minute he was a nobody who at best got the roles that the A-list actors rejected. The next minute he was Hollywood's "Golden Boy" and people couldn't get enough of him. He protested in an interview, "That's not what I signed up to do. This shameless self-promotion is antithetical to acting. That's what I do. I'm just looking forward to getting back to work."

At the end of an already hectic year, Matt committed to yet another film project. In the movie *Rounders*, Matt would be working with an up-and-coming young actor named Edward

In 1998, Matt worked with Edward Norton making the movie Rounders, *about a young professional gambler. During a break in their schedule, the two actors tried their luck at the 19th Annual World Series of Poker, where Matt prepares to play a hand (pictured above). Neither actor did well against the real pros.*

Norton, as well as such respected and talented veterans as Martin Landau, John Malkovich, and John Turturro. The film, which focused on a young professional gambler played by Matt, was about as different from his previous roles as he could get.

By any standard of measurement, 1998 was an extraordinary year for Matt. Besides winning a Golden Globe and an Oscar, he was honored as the "Male Star of Tomorrow" by the ShoWest Society, a group of film directors, actors, and producers. Despite feeling under the weather, Matt appeared at the awards ceremony in Las Vegas. In thanking the society, Matt said, "It's been an amazing year for me and I'm totally grateful to ShoWest and the exhibitors for this vote of confidence in my work."

Good Will Hunting also received nominations from the Screen Actors Guild for Best Actor, Best Supporting Actor, Best Supporting Actress, and Outstanding Cast Performance. (Only Robin Williams won for Best Supporting Actor.) Matt was nominated for Favorite Male Performer at the 4th Annual Blockbuster Awards but lost to Leonardo DiCaprio. The last round of award ceremonies came in June with the MTV Movie Awards, where Matt again finished second to DiCaprio for Favorite Male in a Drama. Matt and Ben were nominated for Best Onscreen Duo, and Matt and his one-time girlfriend, Minnie Driver, were named in the Best Onscreen Kiss Category.

As Matt's professional life blossomed in 1998, so did his personal life. Minnie Driver was only one of the leading actresses Matt romanced. He also dated Claire Danes, his costar in *The Rainmaker*, Elite model Kara Sands, and most recently, actress Winona Ryder. Just as when

he was in high school, Matt's charm and good looks have won him many female fans the world over.

By the summer of 1998, there was no stopping the Matt frenzy. In the spring he had agreed to play the lead role in the film version of Cormac McCarthy's novel *All the Pretty Horses*, directed by Billy Bob Thornton and scheduled for release in 2000. The casting choice was not lost on the industry. Thornton, also an actor, ignited his career when he wrote his own Oscar-winning screenplay, for the 1996 film *Sling Blade*. After finishing work on *Rounders*, Matt flew to

Matt was showered with awards for his work in Good Will Hunting, *including Male Star of Tomorrow, presented at the 24th Annual ShoWest Awards ceremony.*

Matt's surge of popularity carried him into 1999. Here he is shown appearing on The Oprah Winfrey Show *with Gwyneth Paltrow, discussing the movie* The Talented Mr. Ripley, *in which both young actors starred.*

Italy to begin filming what he described as the "most unconventional movie I've done," *The Talented Mr. Ripley.*

Taking time out from his feverish schedule in May 1998, Matt and his *Rounders* costar Edward Norton decided to see how well they could do in the high-stakes world of professional poker. Joining 350 other players, the two entered the World Series of Poker held annually in Las Vegas. Before a room crowded with star-struck fans, Matt and Edward soon discovered the limits of their card-playing abilities. Norton was gone from the table in two hours. Matt did not fare much better: he only lasted for three hours. Matt admitted later, "We never once entertained the fantasy of actually winning." Norton disagreed, saying, "Speak for yourself."

In addition to their many individual film projects, Matt and Ben were always looking for opportunities to work together again. They discussed taking roles in *Halfway House*, a film about workers and residents in a home for the mentally impaired. They also signed to work with director Kevin Smith in *Dogma*, a controversial comedy about two misfit angels who settle in Wisconsin after being cast out of heaven. The film chronicles their efforts to return to paradise.

Despite their success and celebrity, Matt and Ben haven't forgotten their roots. When a donor offered their alma mater, the Cambridge Rindge and Latin School, $10,000 for an autographed photo of the duo, Matt and Ben were quick to oblige. A spokeswoman for the school applauded their generosity, saying, "They could have blown us off and they didn't. And we're $10,000 richer for it."

In July, Matt and Ben were the recipients of the Humanitas Prize, given to the film and television scripts that best "communicate those values which most enrich the human person." The award, bestowed for the script of *Good Will Hunting*, includes a stipend of $25,000.

Meanwhile, film offers kept pouring in. Matt said in an interview that 1998 "was amazing. These movies kind of tumbled one on another— and I've never had that experience. I haven't stopped working since last August. Amazing. Although there is that old joke: What are the two worst times in an actor's life? When he's working and when he's not working!"

Matt now commands close to $5 million a picture, making him one of the highest paid actors in Hollywood. Despite his high salary, the offers just keep coming. At the moment, Matt is being considered for the role of baseball legend Mickey Mantle in a proposed film about the slugger's life. Director Steven Spielberg is also hoping to work with Matt again in the futuristic film *Minority Report*, in which Tom Cruise is slated to star. In a radical departure from his usual film roles, Matt would play the villain in *Minority Report*, scheduled for release in 2000. Matt has signed on for a role in Robert Redford's new golf film, *The Legend of Bagger Vance*. The film, also scheduled for release in 2000, will pair Matt with another box-office sensation, Will Smith. Smith will play the role of a caddy to Matt's character, a World War I veteran and golfer.

Matt and Ben have also formed their own production company, Pearl Street Productions, and have begun work together on a project entitled *The Third Wheel*. This time Ben will get to play the lead role, while Matt will make only a brief cameo appearance. The film will also mark Matt and Ben's debut as executive producers. As if acting and producing were not enough to occupy his time, Matt has stepped from in front of the camera and settled behind the microphone, lending his vocal talents to the animated science fiction film *Titan A.E.*, to be released in 2000.

Following what he jokingly refers to as the "Spam years," Matt is learning to enjoy the rewards of his success. He is not shy about spending money. Recent acquisitions include the purchase of a complete wardrobe for himself and new cars for both of his parents. He and Ben are exploring the possibility of building houses next door to each other somewhere in the Hollywood Hills.

Matt's current status in Hollywood is enviable. Chances are good that if Matt passes on a film project, the film probably won't be made. He now enjoys the luxury of picking and choosing which films he wants to do from the many scripts sent to him. Following up on the success of *Good Will Hunting*, Matt also has plans to write other screenplays. "As a writer, you can really use your creative energy and channel it when you need to do it," as opposed to acting in which "you have no say as to when you have to go to work." He is also thinking seriously about one day trying his hand at directing.

For Matt—actor, screenwriter, producer—the possibilities are limitless, and the future could not be any brighter. Matt's peers and colleagues see in him the potential to become an actor on the level of Jack Nicholson, one of Matt's idols. One director has gone on record stating that "I hope . . . [Matt and his generation of actors] will do what Jack Nicholson did—take one risky role after another and keep taking chances."

No matter what he accomplishes, however, Matt has made a promise to himself that he will never forget who he is or where he comes from— a promise that his family intends to help him keep. "My family doesn't let me get away with anything. They bring me back down to earth and make me realize that my fame doesn't absolve me of being a good human being in any way."

In the years ahead Matt will no doubt work hard to perfect his acting and writing skills. The little boy in the superhero cape has already come a long way in a short time. Frustration and failure have left their mark, but neither has erased Matt's gratitude at the wonderful achievements or his desire to accomplish even more. "My life has definitely turned into an embarrassment of riches," he acknowledged with characteristic modesty. "It's every dream I've ever dared dream come true."

CHRONOLOGY

1970   Born on October 8 in Boston, Massachusetts.

1972   Parents divorce.

1980   Moves to Cambridge, Massachusetts; meets Ben Affleck.

1988   Appears in first movie, *Mystic Pizza;* enters Harvard.

1992   Takes play-writing classes at Harvard; writes first play, which later is revised and becomes the script for *Good Will Hunting;* moves to Los Angeles; begins reworking *Good Will Hunting* with Ben Affleck.

1994   With Affleck, sells *Good Will Hunting* to Castle Rock Entertainment.

1996   Miramax buys *Good Will Hunting* from Castle Rock Entertainment.

1998   Wins Golden Globe Award and Academy Award for Best Original Screenplay for *Good Will Hunting.*

1999   Stars in *Dogma* and *The Talented Mr. Ripley;* receives Golden Globe Best Actor in a Drama nomination for *The Talented Mr. Ripley;* forms production company, Pearl Street Productions, with Ben; works on *The Third Wheel* with Ben as executive producers; records vocal appearance in *Titan A.E.*

ACCOMPLISHMENTS

Filmography

1988	*Mystic Pizza*
	The Good Mother (uncredited)
1992	*School Ties*
1993	*Geronimo: An American Legend*
	Younger and Younger (uncredited)
1996	*Courage Under Fire*
	Glory Daze
1997	*Chasing Amy*
	Good Will Hunting
	The Rainmaker
1998	*Rounders*
	Saving Private Ryan
1999	*Dogma*
	The Talented Mr. Ripley
2000	*All the Pretty Horses*
	The Legend of Bagger Vance
	Titan A.E. (voice)

Television

1990	*Rising Son*
1995	*The Good Old Boys*

Screenplay

1994	*Good Will Hunting* (with Ben Affleck)

AWARDS

1998   Academy Award: Best Original Screenplay for *Good Will Hunting* with Ben Affleck

Golden Globe Award: Best Original Screenplay for *Good Will Hunting* with Ben Affleck

ShoWest Award: Male Star of Tomorrow

Humanitas Prize: Given to the film and television scripts that "best communicate those values which most enrich the human person" for *Good Will Hunting* with Ben Affleck

FURTHER READING

Altman, Sheryl, and Sheryl Berk. *Matt Damon and Ben Affleck: On and Off Screen.* New York: HarperCollins, 1998.

Bego, Mark. *Matt Damon: Chasing a Dream.* New York: Andrews McMeel Publishing, 1998.

Damon, Matt and Ben Affleck. *Good Will Hunting: A Screenplay.* Los Angeles: Talk Miramax Books, 1997.

Diamond, Maxine. *Matt Damon: A Biography.* New York: Pocket Books, 1998.

Nickson, Chris. *Matt Damon: An Unauthorized Biography.* Los Angeles: Renaissance Books, 1999.

Robb, Brian. *The Matt Damon Album.* Medford, NJ: Plexus Publishing, 1999.

Scott, Kieran. *Matt Damon.* New York: Alladin Paperbacks, 1998.

Tracy, Kathleen. *Matt Damon: Hollywood's Hottest Young Superstar.* New York: St. Martin's Press, 1998.

ABOUT THE AUTHOR

MEG GREENE earned a bachelor's degree in history at Lindenwood College in St. Charles, Missouri, and master's degrees from the University of Nebraska at Omaha and the University of Vermont. Ms. Greene is the author of three other books, writes regularly for *Cobblestone Magazine* and other publications, and serves as a contributing editor for *Suite101.com*'s "History for Children." She makes her home in Virginia.

INDEX